ES CALENDAR OF EVENTS

ptember/October 2000	13 W	14 T	15 F	16 S	17 S	18 M	19 T	20 W	21 T	22 F	23 S	24 S	25 M	26 T	27 W	28 T	29 F	30 S	1 S
Football	•	•										•	•		•	•	•	•	
mnastics																			
Rhythmic																	•	•	•
Artistic				•	•	•	•	•	•	•		•	•	*					
Trampoline									•	•									
Handball				•	•	•	•	•	•						•	•	•	•	•
Hockey				•	•	•	•	•	•	•	•	•	•	•	•	•	•	•	
Judo				•	•	•	•	•	•										
Modern Pentathlon																		•	•
Rowing					•	•	•	•	•	•	•	•							
Sailing				•	•	•	•	•	•	•	•	•	•	•	•	•	•	•	
Shooting				•	•	•	•	•	•	•	•								
Softball					•	•	•	•	•	•		•	•		•				
Table Tennis				•	•	•	•	•	•	•									
Taekwondo															•	•	•	•	
Tennis							•	•	•	•	•	•	•	•	•	•			
Triathlon				•	•														
eyball																			
Beach Volleyball				•	•	•	•			•	•	•	•	•					
Volleyball				•	•	•	•	•	•	•	•	•	•	•	•	•	•	•	•
Weightlifting				•	•	•	•	•		•	•	•	•	•					
Wrestling																			
Freestyle															•	•	•	•	
Greco-Roman													•	•	•	•			

on-medal exhibition event

'The most important thing in the Olympic Games is not winning, but taking part; the essential thing in life is not conquering, but fighting well.'

Pierre de Coubertin

Sports Quotations, Maxims, Quips and Pronouncements for Writers and Fans, Andrew J. Maikovich, McFarland & Company, Inc. Publishers, London, 1984.

Sydney 2000 Olympic Games

Host cities of the Modern Olympic Games

OLYMPIAD	YEAR	CITY	NO. OF NATIONS	NO. OF SPORTS
I	1896	ATHENS	13	9
II	1900	PARIS	22	17
III	1904	ST LOUIS	12	14
	1906	ATHENS*		
IV	1908	LONDON	23	21
V	1912	STOCKHOLM	28	13
VI	1916	BERLIN (not held**)		
VII	1920	ANTWERP	29	21
VIII	1924	PARIS	44	18
IX	1928	AMSTERDAM	46	14
X	1932	LOS ANGELES	37	14
XI	1936	BERLIN	49	19
XII	1940	TOKYO/HELSINKI (not held**)		
XIII	1944	LONDON (not held**)		
XIV	1948	LONDON	59	17
XV	1952	HELSINKI	69	17
XVI	1956	MELBOURNE	67	17
XVII	1960	ROME	83	17
XVIII	1964	TOKYO	93	19
XIX	1968	MEXICO CITY	112	18
XX	1972	MUNICH	122	21
XXI	1976	MONTREAL	92	21
XXII	1980	MOSCOW	81	21
XXIII	1984	LOS ANGELES	142	21
XXIV	1988	SEOUL	159	23
XXV	1992	BARCELONA	172	25
XXVI	1996	ATLANTA	197	26
XXVII	2000	SYDNEY	199	28
XXVIII	2004	ATHENS		

* The 1906 Games were the first and only interim Olympic Games

** Games in these years were not held due to war

Contents

History of the Olympic Games 4
Sydney 2000 6
Torch Ceremony 8

Aquatics
  Diving 9
  Swimming 11
  Synchronized Swimming 14
  Water Polo 15
Archery 16
Athletics 17
Badminton 26
Baseball 27
Basketball 28
Boxing 29
Canoe/Kayak
  Slalom 31
  Sprint 32
Cycling
  Mountain bike 33
  Road 33
  Track 34
Equestrian
  Dressage 35
  Jumping 35
  Three Day Event 36
Fencing 37

Football 39
Gymnastics
  Artistic 40
  Rhythmic 40
  Trampoline 41
Handball 44
Hockey 45
Judo 46
Modern Pentathlon 48
Rowing 49
Sailing 51
Shooting 52
Softball 53
Table Tennis 54
Taekwondo 55
Tennis 56
Triathlon 57
Volleyball
  Beach Volleyball 58
  Volleyball 59
Weightlifting 60
Wrestling 62

Nation Abbreviations 64
100 Years of Olympic Games Highlights Foldout
Sydney 2000 Olympic Venues Foldout

History of the Olympic Games

Ancient Olympic Games

The first Games held at Olympia in ancient Greece over 3000 years ago were religious ceremonies in honour of the Greek god Zeus. Young men raced a distance of about 185 metres, the length of a stadium.

The first recorded Olympic Games were held in 766 BC. Although there was only one event – a sprint over about 200 metres – other events were added in later years. Men competed in chariot racing, wrestling, boxing, bareback horse-riding, a pentathlon or a variety of foot races. In one race, contestants had to run wearing a full set of armour.

The ancient Games were held for over 1000 years. After the Romans conquered Greece, battles between slaves and animals became part of the competition. The Games were eventually banned in AD 394 by the Roman Emperor Theodosius. Fifteen hundred years were to pass before the Olympic spirit would be celebrated once more.

Modern Olympic Games

The Modern Olympic Games owe their existence to the vision of a Frenchman, Baron Pierre de Coubertin.

During his travels around the world, he noticed that people from many different countries were interested in sport. In 1894 he arranged a meeting of people from nine countries to talk about the idea of athletes from all over the world participating in a friendly competition. The group became the first International Olympic Committee.

Baron Pierre de Coubertin

Two years later, the first Modern Olympic Games were held in Athens, with 311 male competitors from 13 nations. At the next Olympic Games, in 1900, the men-only rule was changed, and 19 women athletes joined the competition.

Runners line up at the first Modern Olympic Games in 1896.

Sydney 2000

15 September to 1 October

The host for the 2000 Olympic Games is the shining harbour city of Sydney. Sydney is the capital of New South Wales, on the eastern coast of Australia.

The Games will begin with the Opening Ceremony on Friday 15 September and continue for 16 days. Twenty-eight sports will be contested by over 10 000 athletes.

Events will be held in a variety of venues in and around Sydney, including the Olympic Stadium, International Aquatic Centre and SuperDome at Sydney Olympic Park, Penrith Lakes, Centennial Parklands, Bondi Beach and the Exhibition Halls at Darling Harbour.

Torch Ceremony

The Sydney 2000 Olympic Torch Relay will offer Australians a unique opportunity to share the spirit of the Olympic Games. The torch will be lit on 10 May from a flame kindled by the sun's rays at a special ceremony in Olympia, Greece, home of the original Olympic Games. From there the torch will be carried by various means of transport to Sydney, visiting 13 Olympic nations in Oceania on the way.

Once within Australia, the torch will visit all States and Territories. Ten thousand Torchbearers, including Olympians, community representatives and people from all walks of life, will each run for up to one kilometre carrying the torch. It will also travel by other forms of transport, including a tram, stock horse, dragon boat, solar car and the Royal Flying Doctor Service.

After 100 days of travel around Australia the torch will arrive at the Olympic Stadium in Sydney on 15 September, in time for the Opening Ceremony.

Aquatics

Diving

Diving originated with European gymnasts performing on beaches. Diving became a recognised sport in the 19th century, and first featured on the Olympic program in St Louis in 1904.

The Olympic program consists of 10 metre platform and 3 metre springboard individual and synchronized events for men and women. Synchronized diving is a new Olympic event.

Mingxia Fu (CHN), Olympic gold medallist at Atlanta.

Individual events

Competitors can choose to perform dives from a list of dives that have been rated according to their degree of difficulty, or they can create their own. Points are awarded for approach, take-off, elevation, execution of movements and entry into the water.

VENUE
Sydney International Aquatic
Centre, Sydney Olympic Park

Synchronized diving

The pairs must perform a combination of dives. These must be perfectly timed for height and distance from the board or platform, speed of rotation, and angle of entry into the water.

Australian Synchronized diving champions Matthew Helm and Tony Lawson.

Men's events

Event	1996 winner	2000 winner
3 m Springboard	Ni Xiong (CHN)	
10 m Platform	Dmitri Sautin (RUS)	
Synch. 3 m springboard	New event	
Synch. 10 m platform	New event	

Women's events

Event	1996 winner	2000 winner
3 m Springboard	Mingxia Fu (CHN)	
10 m Platform	Mingxia Fu (CHN)	
Synch. 3 m springboard	New event	
Synch. 10 m platform	New event	

Swimming

Swimming has been an important part of the Olympic Games since 1896 when four events for men were held in open waters at the Bay of Zea in Athens. The races included a 100 metres freestyle for sailors. Women's events were added to the program in 1912.

The Olympic swimming program today includes events for freestyle, backstroke, breaststroke and butterfly, with all four strokes being used in medley events.

The pools at the Sydney International Aquatic Centre have wave-killing gutters and lane markers that have been designed to reduce turbulence. The use of hi-tech equipment such as electronics in starting blocks and touch pads means that race results can now be automatically timed to a hundredth of a second.

Kieren Perkins (AUS) wins gold in 1996 for the 1500 m freestyle.

Penelope Heyns (RSA), gold medallist at Atlanta for both 100 m and 200 m breaststroke.

11

Men's events

Event	Olympic record and time	1996 winner and time	2000 winner and time
50 m freestyle	Alexander Popov (CIS) 21.91	Alexander Popov (RUS) 22.13	....
100 m freestyle	Matt Biondi (USA) 48.63	Alexander Popov (RUS) 48.74	....
200 m freestyle	Yevgeniy Sadovyi (CIS) 1:46.70	Danyon Loader (NZL) 1:47.63	....
400 m freestyle	Yevgeniy Sadovyi (CIS) 3:45.00	Danyon Loader (NZL) 3:47.97	....
1500 m freestyle	Kieren Perkins (AUS) 14:43.48	Kieren Perkins (AUS) 14:56.40	....
100 m backstroke	Jeff Rouse (USA) 53.86	Jeff Rouse (USA) 54.10	....
200 m backstroke	Martin Lopez-Zubero (ESP) 1:58.47	Brad Bridgewater (USA) 1:58.54	....
100 m breaststroke	Fred Deburghgraeve (BEL) 1:00.60	Fred Deburghgraeve (BEL) 1:00.65	....
200 m breaststroke	Mike Barrowman (USA) 2:10.16	Norbert Rozsa (HUN) 2:12.57	....
100 m butterfly	Denis Pankratov (RUS) 52.27	Denis Pankratov (RUS) 52.27	....
200 m butterfly	Mel Stewart (USA) 1:56.26	Denis Pankratov (RUS) 1:56.51	....
200 m medley	Attila Czene (HUN) 1:59.91	Attila Czene (HUN) 1:59.91	....
400 m medley	Tamas Darnyi (HUN) 4:14.23	Tom Dolan (USA) 4:14.90	....
4x100 m freestyle	USA 3:15.41	USA 3:15.41	....
4x200 m freestyle	CIS 7:11.95	USA 7:14.84	....
4x100 m medley	USA 3:34.84	USA 3:34.84	....

Women's events

Event	Olympic record and time	1996 winner and time	2000 winner and time
50 m freestyle	Wenyi Yang (CHN) 24.79	Amy van Dyken (USA) 24.87	....
100 m freestyle	Jingyi Yang (CHN) 54.50	Jingyi Yang (CHN) 54.50	....
200 m freestyle	Heike Friedrich (GDR) 1:57.65	Claudia Poll (CRC) 1:58.16	....
400 m freestyle	Janet Evans (USA) 4:03.85	Michelle Smith (IRL) 4:07.25	....
800 m freestyle	Janet Evans (USA) 8:20.20	Brooke Bennett (USA) 8:27.89	....
100 m backstroke	Krisztina Egerszegi (HUN) 1:00.68	Beth Botsford (USA) 1:01.19	....
200 m backstroke	Krisztina Egerszegi (HUN) 2:07.06	Krisztina Egerszegi (HUN) 2:07.83	....
100 m breaststroke	Penelope Heyns (RSA) 1:07.02	Penelope Heyns (RSA) 1:07.73	....
200 m breaststroke	Penelope Heyns (RSA) 2:25.41	Penelope Heyns (RSA) 2:25.41	....
100 m butterfly	Hong Qian (CHN) 58.62	Amy van Dyken (USA) 59.13	....
200 m butterfly	Mary T. Meagher (USA) 2:06.90	Susan O'Neill (AUS) 2:07.76	....
200 m medley	Li Lin (CHN) 2:11.65	Michelle Smith (IRL) 2:13.93	....
400 m medley	Petra Schneider (GDR) 4:36.29	Michelle Smith (IRL) 4:39.18	....
4x100 m freestyle	USA 3:39.46	USA 3:39.46	....
4x200 m freestyle	USA 7:59.87	USA 7:59.87	....
4x100 m medley	USA 4:02.54	USA 4:02.88	....

Synchronized Swimming

Synchronized swimming was once referred to as 'water ballet'. Its demanding routines require competitors to possess a variety of skills, including endurance, strength, flexibility, artistry and exceptional breath control. The program at Sydney will consist of duet and team.

A duet perfectly 'in synch'.

Synchronized swimming

	1996 winner	2000 winner
Team	USA	....
Duet	New event	....

Water Polo

Water polo was created by the London Swimming Club in 1870. The concept was to develop a 'football-like game in water'. The game first appeared on the program in Paris in 1900. Women's water polo becomes an Olympic sport for the first time this year.

Water polo is such a demanding sport that players need to be exceptionally fit. The game is played over four seven-minute periods. To score, players must throw the ball into their opponents' goal.

OLYMPIC FACT

Water polo players can swim as far as five kilometres during a game, and are not allowed to touch the bottom of the pool during play.

Igor Hinic (CRO), the Atlanta 1996 Olympic Games silver medallist.

Events

Event	1996 winner	2000 winner
Men's	Spain	
Women's	New event	

Archery

Bows and arrows have been used for centuries for both hunting and sport. Archery became an Olympic event in 1900.

INDIVIDUAL EVENTS

In the first round of competition, the archers each fire 72 arrows at the target and are given a ranking from one to 64. They then compete in head-to-head matches until the winner is decided. Archers in the finals round each fire 12 arrows, with the archer who achieves the best score advancing to the next round.

Justin Huish (USA), gold medallist at Atlanta.

TEAM EVENTS

In the finals round of team events, each archer fires nine arrows at the target. The combined total of each team's 27 arrows decides the winner.

Events

Men's	1996 winner	2000 winner
Individual	Justin Huish (USA)	
Team	USA	
Women's		
Individual	Kim Kyung-Wook (KOR)	
Team	Korea	

VENUE
Archery Centre, Sydney Olympic Park

Athletics

Athletic events are the most popular part of the Olympic program. They attract more competitors from more countries than any other Olympic sport. Track races have been a part of every Olympic Games.

Track events

TRACK RACES

The 100 metre sprint is one of the most exciting events at the Olympic Games. The winners are among the fastest runners in the world.

The Olympic running track is divided into eight lanes. Each lap is 400 metres. The 100 metre sprint is run on a straight section of the track. The 200, 400 and 800 metre races have staggered starts so that each competitor runs an equal distance.

Competitors in the 200 metre and 400 metre run in lanes for the complete distance, but the 800 metre competitors cross to the inside lane after 100 metres.

Sprints: 100 m, 200 m, 400 m
Middle distance: 800 m, 1500 m, 5000 m
Distance Events: 10 000 m

Donovan Bailey (CAN) on his way to gold for the 100 m at the Atlanta 1996 Olympic Games.

VENUE
The Olympic Stadium, Sydney Olympic Park

Svetlana Masterkova (RUS) won both the 800 m and 1500 m at Atlanta.

MARATHON

The men's marathon dates back to 490 BC, and has been run at every Modern Olympic Games. Women first ran the marathon at the Los Angeles Olympic Games in 1984. In Sydney 2000, the course will start at North Sydney. Runners will cross the Harbour Bridge before winding their way through central Sydney and heading out to the Olympic Stadium.

Fatuma Roba (ETH), the Atlanta 1996 Olympic Games women's marathon champion.

WALK

In walking races, athletes must touch the ground with their front foot before their back foot leaves the ground. Top walkers reach speeds of up to 15 kilometres per hour. Road walking will take place around Sydney Olympic Park, starting and finishing in the Olympic Stadium.

Marathon: 42.195 km
Walk: 20 km, 50 km

HURDLES AND STEEPLECHASE

Hurdling is one of the most skillful track events, requiring a mixture of speed and balance. Hurdlers need to jump ten 'flights' in each race. These vary in height from 0.76 metres to 1.67 metres, depending on the event. The 400 metre event is so physically demanding, it is known as the 'man killer'.

In the men's 3000 metre steeplechase event, runners race along an obstacle course containing 28 solid hurdles and seven water jumps.

> **Men's steeplechase: 300 m**
> **Men's hurdles: 110 m, 400 m**
> **Women's hurdles: 100 m, 400 m**

RELAYS

Relay teams have four runners, who each run a leg of the race before passing the baton on to the next runner. The baton must be exchanged within the 10-metre-long change-over zone or the team will be disqualified.

> **Men's and women's relays:**
> **4 x 100 m, 4 x 400 m**

Gail Devers (USA) competes in the women's hurdles.

19

Men's track events

Event	Olympic record and time	1996 winner and time	2000 winner and time
100 m	Donovan Bailey (CAN) 9.84	Donovan Bailey (CAN) 9.94	
200 m	Michael Johnson (USA) 19.32	Michael Johnson (USA) 19.32	
400 m	Michael Johnson (USA) 43.49	Michael Johnson (USA) 43.49	
800 m	Vebjoern Rodal (NOR) 1:42.58	Vebjoern Rodal (NOR) 1:42.58	
1500 m	Sebastian Coe (GBR) 3:32.53	Noureddine Morceli (ALG) 3:35.78	
5000 m	Said Aouita (MAR) 13:05.59	Venuste Nyongabo (BDI) 13:07.96	
10 000 m	Haile Gebrselassie (ETH) 27:07.34	Haile Gebrselassie (ETH) 27:07.34	
Marathon	Carlos Lopes (POR) 2:09:21	Josiah Thugwane (RSA) 2:12:36	
110 m hurdles	Allen Johnson (USA) 12.95	Allen Johnson (USA) 12.95	
400 m hurdles	Kevin Young (USA) 46.78	Derrick Adkins (USA) 47.54	
3000 m s/chase	Julius Karioki (KEN) 8:05.51	Joseph Keter (KEN) 8:07.12	
4 x 100 m relay	USA 37.40	Canada 37.69	
4 x 400 m relay	USA 2:55.74	USA 2:55.99	
20 km walk	Josef Pribilinec (TCH) 1:19:57	Jefferson Perez (ECU) 1:20:07	
50 km walk	Vyacheslav Ivanenko (URS) 3:38:29	Robert Korzeniowski (POL) 3:43:30	

Women's track events

Event	Olympic record and time	1996 winner and time	2000 winner and time
100 m	Florence G-Joyner (USA) 10.62	Gail Devers (USA) 10.94	
200 m	Florence G-Joyner (USA) 21.34	Marie-José Perec (FRA) 22.12	
400 m	Marie-José Perec (FRA) 48.25	Marie-José Perec (FRA) 48.25	
800 m	Nadezhda Olizarenko (URS) 1:53.43	Svetlana Masterkova (RUS) 1:57.73	
1500 m	Paula Ivan (ROM) 3:53.96	Svetlana Masterkova (RUS) 4:00.83	
5000 m	Junxia Wang (CHN) 14:59.88	Junxia Wang (CHN) 14:59.88	
10 000 m	Fernanda Ribeiro (POR) 31:01.64	Fernanda Ribeiro (POR) 31:01.64	
Marathon	Joan Benoit (USA) 2:24:52	Fatuma Roba (ETH) 2:26:05	
100 m hurdles	Yordanka Donkova (BUL) 12.38	Lyudmila Engquist (SWE) 12.58	
400 m hurdles	Deon Hemmings (JAM) 52.82	Deon Hemmings (JAM) 52.82	
4 x 100 m relay	GDR 41.60	USA 41.95	
4 x 400 m relay	URS 3:15.17	USA 3:20.91	
20 km walk	New event		

> **Track demonstration events:**
> **Men's wheelchair: 1500 m**
> **Women's wheelchair: 800 m**

Field events

JUMPING EVENTS

High Jump

High jumping was part of the ancient Greek Olympic Games. Jumpers can choose any style to clear the bar, as long as they start off from one foot. If jumpers miss clearing the bar three times in a row, they are eliminated. The bar is raised until all the athletes have reached their limit.

Charles Austin (USA) takes gold at Atlanta for the men's high jump.

Pole Vault

Athletes use a fibreglass pole to help push themselves over the bar, legs first and face down. The rules are similar to those for High Jump.

Long Jump

This event was held at the first Modern Olympic Games. A women's event was added to the program in 1948. Jumpers must not step over the edge of the take-off board nearest the sand pit, or they will end up with a 'no jump'. A jump is measured from the take-off board to the nearest mark made by the ahtlete's body in the sand pit.

Triple Jump

Also known as the 'hop, step and jump', the Triple Jump is thought to have developed from hopscotch. This event has similar rules to the Long Jump, except for the placement of feet in the hopping phase.

THROWING EVENTS

Athletes are given three attempts to qualify for the final. If they step out of the circle (or over the line for the javelin) while throwing, they are disqualified.

Shot Put

A shot must be lifted from the athlete's shoulder, rather than thrown.

> Men's: 7.26 kg
> Women's: 4 kg

Discus Throw

Discus Throw was one of the main events at the ancient Olympic Games. Each athlete is allowed three throws with the top eight given an extra three.

> Men's: 2 kg, 22 cm diameter
> Women's: 1 kg, 18 cm diameter

Hammer Throw

A protective 'cage' is placed around the hammer thrower in case the hammer flies wild and harms spectators.

> Metal ball: 7.26 kg
> Steel wire and handle:
> 121.5 cm

Javelin Throw

A javelin must land with its sharp end pointing downwards for the throw to count. Javelins were modified in 1986 to reduce the distance they could be thrown. Javelins were being thrown so far that organisers feared for the safety of spectators and runners on the track.

> Men's javelin: 800 g
> Women's javelin: 600 g

Jan Zelezny (CZE), gold medallist at Atlanta.

MEN'S DECATHLON

The Decathlon is the toughest sport of the Olympic Games and consists of ten events, held over two days. Points are awarded for each section. Medals are awarded to the athletes with the highest overall scores.

> **Day one:** 100 m dash, long jump, shot put, high jump, 400 m run
> **Day two:** 110 m hurdles, discus, pole vault, javelin, 1500 m run

Men's field events

Event	Olympic record and time	1996 winner and time	2000 winner and time
High jump	Charles Austin (USA) 2.39 m	Charles Austin (USA) 2.39 m	
Pole vault	Jean Galfione (FRA) 5.92 m	Jean Galfione (FRA) 5.92 m	
Long jump	Bob Beamon (USA) 8.90 m	Carl Lewis (USA) 8.50 m	
Triple jump	Kenny Harrison (USA) 18.09 m	Kenny Harrison (USA) 18.09 m	
Shot put	Ulf Timmermann (GDR) 22.47 m	Randy Barnes (USA) 21.62 m	
Discus	Lars Riedel (GER) 69.40 m	Lars Riedel (GER) 69.40 m	
Javelin	Jan Zelezny (CZE) 89.66 m	Jan Zelezny (CZE) 88.16 m	
Hammer	Sergey Litvinov (URS) 84.80 m	Balazs Kiss (HUN) 81.24 m	
Decathlon	Daley Thompson (GBR) 8847 pts	Dan O'Brien (USA) 8824 pts	

WOMEN'S HEPTATHLON

The Heptathlon replaced the five-event Pentathlon at the 1984 Los Angeles Games. Although it has three less events, its structure and scoring system is similar to the Decathlon.

Chioma Ajunwa (NGR) leaps to gold in the women's long jump at the Atlanta 1996 Olympic Games.

Day one: 100 m hurdles, shot put, high jump, 200 m run
Day two: long jump, javelin, 800 m run

- New events for 2000 are the women's pole vault and hammer throw.

Women's field events

Event	Olympic record and time	1996 winner and time	2000 winner and time
High jump	Stefka Kostadinova (BUL) 2.05 m	Stefka Kostadinova (BUL) 2.05 m	
Pole vault	New event		
Long jump	Jackie J-Kersee (USA) 7.40 m	Chioma Ajunwa (NGR) 7.12 m	
Triple jump	Inessa Kravets (UKR) 15.33 m	Inessa Kravets (UKR) 15.33 m	
Shot put	Ilona Slupianek (GDR) 22.41 m	Astrid Kumbernuss (GER) 20.56 m	
Discus	Martina Hellman (GDR) 72.30 m	Ilke Wyludda (GER) 69.66 m	
Javelin	Petra Felke (GDR) 74.68 m	Heli Rantanen (NOR) 67.94 m	
Hammer	New event		
Heptathlon	Jackie J-Kersee (USA) 7291 pts	Ghada Shouaa (SYR) 6780 pts	

Badminton

Badminton is the world's fastest racquet sport. British officers in India in the 1800s played a modern version of the game, called 'Poona'. The name changed when they played the game at Badminton – the estate of the English Duke of Beaufort.

The Malaysian team on their way to silver at Atlanta.

Badminton became an Olympic sport in 1992 where men's and women's singles and doubles were introduced. Mixed doubles were introduced in 1996. In men's singles and doubles events, and in mixed doubles, the first player or team to score 15 points wins the game. In women's singles, it is the first to score 11 points. Only the serving side can win points.

Events

Event	1996 winner	2000 winner
Men's singles	Poul-Erik Hoyer-Larsen (DEN)	
Men's doubles	Rexy Mainaky/Ricky Subagja (INA)	
Women's singles	Bang Soo-Hyun (KOR)	
Women's doubles	Ge Fei/Gu Jun (CHN)	
Mixed doubles	Kim Dong-Moon/Gil Young-ah (KOR)	

VENUE
Pavilion 3, Sydney Olympic Park

Baseball

An American invention, baseball is played in 120 countries around the world. A demonstration sport for many years, it became an official Olympic sport for men in 1992. This is the first Olympic Games that the game has been open to professional players.

Eight teams will play a round robin tournament, leading to semifinal and medal games. The game is played on a diamond-shaped field, with a base in each corner. Each team has nine players. Designated hitters – specialist batters who take the place of the pitcher – are allowed in Olympic competition.

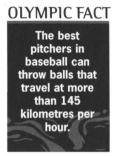

OLYMPIC FACT

The best pitchers in baseball can throw balls that travel at more than 145 kilometres per hour.

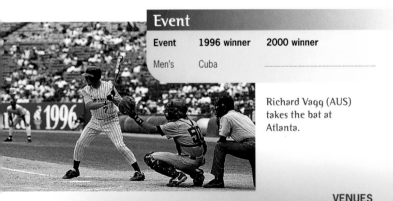

Event

Event	1996 winner	2000 winner
Men's	Cuba	

Richard Vagg (AUS) takes the bat at Atlanta.

VENUES
Baseball Stadium, Sydney Olympic Park;
NSW Baseball Centre, Aquilina Reserve, Blacktown

Basketball

The first Olympic basketball games were played in 1936 on outdoor sand courts which became muddy when it rained during the finals. Now played in indoor stadiums, basketball has become one of the most popular sports on the Olympic program. Women joined the competition in 1976.

Teamwork and strategy are important components of basketball. Each team can have five players on the court at any one time, as well as seven substitute players. The aim of each team is to score into the opponent's basket, and to prevent the other team from securing the ball or scoring.

OLYMPIC FACT

The USA team won every game they played from the time basketball entered Olympic competition in 1936. Their 62-game winning streak was finally halted when they were defeated by the USSR in 1972.

Events

Event	1996 winner	2000 winner
Men's	USA	
Women's	USA	

Shaquille O'Neal (USA), team gold medallist at Atlanta.

VENUES
Preliminary games:
The Dome, Sydney Olympic Park
Quarterfinals and finals:
SuperDome, Sydney Olympic Park

Boxing

Boxing became part of the modern Olympic program in 1904 in St Louis. Only amateur boxers are allowed to compete at the Olympic Games. The main differences between amateur and professional boxing are that amateur boxers wear protective head gear, and the referee is more likely to stop the fight if one of the boxers is receiving heavy punishment. There are no women's events.

A boxing bout can be won by knockout, technical decision, disqualification, retirement or by a points decision made by a panel of five judges. Judges use a computerised scoring system, pushing a button each time a boxer lands a clean punch on his opponent. Three of the five judges must press the button within one second of the punch landing for a point to be awarded.

Somluck Kamsing (THA) takes the gold from Serafim Todorov (BUL) at the Atlanta 1996 Olympic Games.

VENUE
Exhibition Hall 3 (preliminaries) and Hall 4 (finals) at Darling Harbour

Events

Event	1996 winner	2000 winner
Light flyweight (– 48 kg)	Daniel Petrov (BUL)	
Flyweight (– 51 kg)	Maikro Romero (CUB)	
Bantamweight (– 54 kg)	Istvan Kovacs (HUN)	
Featherweight (– 57 kg)	Sornluck Kamsing (THA)	
Lightweight (– 60 kg)	Hocine Soltani (ALG)	
Light W/weight (– 63.5 kg)	Hector Vinent (CUB)	
Welterweight (– 67 kg)	Oleg Saitov (RUS)	
Light M/weight (– 71 kg)	David Reid (USA)	
Middleweight (– 75 kg)	Ariel Hernandez (CUB)	
Light H/weight (– 81 kg)	Vasili Jirov (KAZ)	
Heavyweight (– 91 kg)	Felix Savon (CUB)	
Super H/weight (+ 91 kg)	Vladimir Klichko (UKR)	

OLYMPIC FACT

Seven world heavyweight boxing champions began their careers at the Olympic Games, including Muhammad Ali, Joe Frazier, George Foreman and Evander Holyfield.

David Reid (USA) and Alfredo Duvergel (CUB) battling for the light middleweight gold at the Atlanta 1996 Olympic Games.

Canoe/Kayak

Canoes and kayaks have been used over many thousands of years for hunting and transport. Canoeing/kayaking on a flat-water course became an Olympic sport for men in 1936 and for women in 1948. Whitewater slalom events were added to the Olympic program in 1972.

Canoes are open boats. Competitors kneel in the boats and move them through the water using single-bladed paddles. Kayaks are closed boats, and the paddles have blades at both ends. Competitors use their feet to control a rudder that steers the boat.

Michal Martikan (SVK) takes gold in a 1996 slalom event.

Slalom events

Competitors work their way downstream along a course of rapidly moving water, passing through a series of gates. The course is approximately 300 metres long. The competitor with the fastest combined time over two runs wins.

PENALTIES

Touching a gate: 2 seconds.
Missing a gate completely: 50 seconds.

VENUES
Sprint events: Sydney International Regatta Centre, Penrith Lakes
Slalom events: Penrith Whitewater Stadium, Penrith Lakes

Sprint events

Canoe/kayak sprint events are held on flat water over 500 and 1000 metres. Medals are awarded for the fastest times.

Events

SLALOM

Men's	1996 winner	2000 winner
Kayak single (K1M)	Oliver Fix (GER)	
Canoe single (C1)	Michal Martikan (SVK)	
Canoe double (C2)	France	

Women's		
Kayak Single (K1W)	Stepanka Hilgertova (CZE)	

SPRINT

Men's	1996 winner	2000 winner
Kayak single (K1) 500 m	Antonio Rossi (ITA)	
Kayak double (K2) 500 m	Germany	
Kayak single (K1) 1000 m	Knut Holmann (NOR)	
Kayak double (K2) 1000 m	Italy	
Kayak four (K4) 1000 m	Germany	
Canoe single (C1) 500 m	Martin Doktor (CZE)	
Canoe double (C2) 500 m	Hungary	
Canoe single (C1) 1000 m	Martin Doktor (CZE)	
Canoe double (C2) 1000 m	Germany	

Women's		
Kayak single (K1) 500 m	Rita Koban (HUN)	
Kayak double (K2) 500 m	Sweden	
Kayak four (K4) 500 m	Germany	

Cycling

Cycling is one of the toughest events at the Olympic Games. Men's cycling was part of the first Games in 1896, and women's events were added in 1984.

Clara Hughes (CAN) won bronze for both her road race and time trial at the Atlanta 1996 Olympic Games.

Mountain bike

Riders need special handling skills to master the rugged, demanding bushland course. All riders begin the race at the same time. Men race a total of seven laps (40-50 km) and women race a total of five laps (30-40 km).

Road

All riders begin at the same time in the road race. Men race 13 laps of the road circuit (234 km) and women seven laps (126 km). The individual time trial is a race against the clock. Riders start individually, with a 90-second gap between each competitor. Men race three laps (46.8 km) and women two laps (31.2 km).

OLYMPIC FACT

Mountain bike riders are not allowed any outside assistance. They must carry their own spares and tool kits to repair their bikes while on course.

VENUES
Track cycling: Dunc Gray Velodrome, Bankstown
Road events: Centennial Parklands
Mountain bike: Fairfield City Farm

Track

Twelve different events are contested on a velodrome track. Track cycles have only one gear and no brakes. Riders wear sleek 'skin suits' and aerodynamic helmets to maximise their speed. There are four new events this year: the women's 500 metre time trial and the men's keirin, madison and Olympic sprint.

Men's events

Event	1996 winner	2000 winner
1 km time trial	Florian Rousseau (FRA)	
Sprint	Jens Fiedler (GER)	
Olympic sprint	New event	
Madison	New event	
Keirin	New event	
Individual pursuit	Andrea Collinelli (ITA)	
Team pursuit	France	
Points race	Silvio Martinello (ITA)	
Road race	Pascal Richard (SUI)	
Individual time trial	Miguel Indurain (ESP)	
Cross-country	Bart Brentjens (NED)	

Women's events

Event	1996 winner	2000 winner
500 m time trial	New event	
Sprint	Felicia Ballanger (FRA)	
Individual pursuit	Antonella Bellutti (ITA)	
Points race	Nathalie Lancien (FRA)	
Road race	Jeannie Longo-Ciprelli (FRA)	
Individual time trial	Zulfia Zabirova (RUS)	
Cross-country	Paola Pezzo (ITA)	

Equestrian

Equestrian is the only sport in the Olympic Games in which male and female athletes compete against each other on an equal basis. Teams, consisting of three or four riders, can contain either sex.

Dressage

Dressage has been described as 'horses performing ballet'. The horse and rider perform a test that shows the level of control and communication between them. The judges give points out of 10 for each of the 36 set 'movements' the horse performs. These include the varying of each pace, halting and direction changes.

Andrew Nicholson (NZL) guides Jagermeister at Atlanta.

Jumping

The horse and rider jump a series of obstacles in as fast a time as possible. The course may include water jumps, simulated stone walls, parallel rails and triple jumps. Penalty points are added to the score if a horse refuses a jump, knocks down a rail, or if a rider takes jumps in the wrong order or goes over the time limit. Medals are awarded to teams and individual riders.

VENUE
Sydney International Equestrian Centre, Horsley Park

Three Day Event

This event tests the versatility, obedience, jumping ability and endurance of the horse over three days. There are three sections: dressage, cross-country and jumping. The cross-country section has four phases: two sets of roads and tracks, a steeplechase and a cross-country course. The course is made up of obstacles, hills and broken ground.

Ludger Beerbaum (GER), team gold medallist at Atlanta.

OLYMPIC FACT

Although suffering concussion and a broken collarbone from a fall in the endurance test, Australian Bill Roycroft left his hospital bed to compete in the jumping test, ensuring that his team won the gold medal in Rome in 1960. He went on to compete at four more Games.

Events

Event	1996 winner	2000 winner
Three Day Event	Blyth Tait (NZL)	
Three Day Event, team	Australia	
Dressage	Isabell Werth (GER)	
Dressage, team	Germany	
Jumping	Ulrich Kirchhoff (GER)	
Jumping, team	Germany	

Fencing

Fencing has a curious place in Olympic history. It is the first sport to allow professionals to compete for medals. It is one of only four sports that have been featured at every Modern Olympic Games. Women have been competing since 1924. To score points, a competitor must hit certain target areas on their opponent's body. Electronic devices send out a signal each time they score a hit.

swatch TIMING

FOIL

The lightest of the blades used in fencing, the foil has a flexible rectangular blade with a blunt point. Target areas: between the collar and hipbones.

Competitors test their skills at the Atlanta Games in 1996.

VENUE
Exhibition Hall 5
(preliminaries)
and Hall 4 (finals)
at Darling Harbour

SABRE

The sabre has a flexible triangular blade with a blunt point.

Target areas: any part of the body above the waist, including the head.

ÉPÉE

A heavier sword than the foil, its blade is triangular. The first competitor to hit the other scores one point.

Target areas: any part of the body.

Men's events

Event	1996 winner	2000 winner
Individual foil	Alessandro Puccini (ITA)	
Team foil	Russia	
Individual épée	Alexander Beketov (RUS)	
Team épée	Italy	
Individual sabre	Stanislav Pozdnyakov (RUS)	
Team sabre	Russia	

Women's events

Event	1996 winner	2000 winner
Individual foil	Laura Badea (ROM)	
Team foil	Italy	
Individual épée	Laura Flessel (FRA)	
Team épée	France	

Football

Football, also known as soccer, is the most popular sport in the world. It was first played at the Paris Games in 1900. Women's teams became part of the Olympic program at Atlanta in 1996.

Sixteen men's teams and eight women's teams will compete this year. The women's tournament is open to players aged 16 and over. The men's tournament is restricted to players under the age of 23, although each team is allowed to field three older players.

OLYMPIC FACT

Football is likely to attract more spectators than any other event at the Sydney Olympic Games. More than 1.5 million tickets are available for matches at the various interstate venues.

Medal favourites for 2000

Men: Argentina, Nigeria, Brazil, Australia.
Women: USA, China, Norway, Australia.

Events

Event	1996 winner	2000 winner
Men's	Nigeria	
Women's	USA	

Diego Simeone (ARG), silver medallist at the Atlanta 1996 Olympic Games.

VENUES
Brisbane: Brisbane Cricket Ground;
Adelaide: Hindmarsh Stadium;
Canberra: Bruce Stadium; Melbourne: Melbourne Cricket Ground;
Sydney: Olympic Stadium, Sydney Olympic Park
and Sydney Football Stadium, Moore Park

Gymnastics

The ancient Greeks believed that gymnastics was an important part of education, and an excellent preparation for battle. Gymnastic events, including rope climbing, were held at the ancient Olympic Games in honour of the god Zeus. They have been on the program at every Modern Olympic Games.

Artistic gymnastics

All competitors receive marks out of 10 from a panel of judges for each exercise. Optional exercises only are performed.

Yanina Batyrchina (RUS), silver medallist in 1996.

Women's equipment: floor, balance beam, uneven bars and vault. Men's equipment: horizontal bar, parallel bars, rings, pommel horse, vault and floor.

Rhythmic gymnastics

Only women compete in rhythmic gymnastics. There are events for both individuals and groups. In the group event, five

Li Donghua (SUI) on his way to gold on the pommel horse, at the Atlanta 1996 Olympic Games.

gymnasts work together as one unit. They are judged on their ability to perform together as a group, their mastery of the different equipment, and their other gymnastic skills. Group equipment: ribbon, hoop. Individual equipment: rope, hoop, ball, ribbon.

Trampoline

This is a new event at the Olympic Games. The first trampoline was invented by an American, George Nissen, in his garage. Both men and women will compete in individual trampoline.

Events:
Men's individual
Women's individual

VENUES
Artistic gymnastics and trampoline:
SuperDome, Sydney Olympic Park
Rhythmic gymnastics: Pavilion 3,
Sydney Olympic Park

Artistic gymnastics

Men's Events	1996 winner	2000 winner
Floor exercise	Ioannis Melissanidis (GRE)	
Pommel horse	Li Donghua (SUI)	
Rings	Yuri Chechi (ITA)	
Vault	Alexei Nemov (RUS)	
Parallel bars	Rustam Sharipov (UKR)	
Horizontal bar	Andreas Wecker (GER)	
All-round	Li Xiaoshuang (CHN)	
Team event	Russia	

Women's events	1996 winner	2000 winner
Vault	Simona Amanar (ROM)	
Uneven bars	Svetlana Chorkina (RUS)	
Balance beam	Shannon Miller (USA)	
Floor exercise	Lilia Podkopayeva (UKR)	
All-round	Lilia Podkopayeva (UKR)	
Team event	USA	

Lilia Podkopayeva (UKR) won silver for her beam routine at Atlanta.

Soviet Union/Ukrainian gymnast Larissa Latynina holds the record for the greatest number of medals won by one athlete. Over three Olympic Games (Melbourne 1956, Rome 1960 and Tokyo 1964), Latynina won 18 Olympic medals – nine gold, five silver and four bronze.

Yekaterina Serebryanskaya (UKR) competing at Atlanta in 1996.

Special event: A gymnastics gala event, featuring 76 of the world's best gymnasts.

Rhythmic gymnastics

Event	1996 winner	2000 winner
Individual	Yekaterina Serebryanskaya (UKR)	
Group	Spain	

Trampoline

Event	1996 winner	2000 winner
Men's individual	New event	
Women's individual	New event	

Handball

Handball is a fast, exciting team sport which has many similarities to football, except that the players use their feet instead of their hands to score goals.

Field handball, played 11-a-side on a football-sized pitch, became an Olympic sport at Berlin in 1936. Handball was reintroduced to the Olympic program for men at the Munich Games in 1972. A women's competition was added at Montreal in 1976.

The modern game of handball is played indoors on a 40m x 20m court with six players and a goalkeeper in each team. Players move the ball up the court with their hands by passing or dribbling, then throw the ball past the goalkeeper into a 3m x 2m goal.

Players must be outside a six metre arc or in the air and not in contact with the ground when they shoot for goal.

Croatia takes gold from Sweden in 1996.

Events

Event	1996 winner	2000 winner
Men's	Croatia	
Women's	Denmark	

VENUES
Preliminaries and men's
quarterfinals: Pavilion 2, Sydney Olympic Park
All other finals: The Dome, Sydney Olympic Park

Hockey

According to archaeological reports, a form of hockey was first played 4500 years ago in the Nile Valley in Egypt, with sticks and rocks. Hockey became an Olympic sport for men in 1908, and for women in 1980.

Hockey is played by two teams of 11 players, including a goalkeeper. Each match has two 35-minute halves. Players must be inside the shooting circle to shoot for goal. Free hits are awarded to players by the umpire when rules are broken.

Members of the gold-winning Australian team battling for the ball at the Atlanta 1996 Olympic Games.

OLYMPIC FACT

Australia is one of the strongest hockey nations in the world. The Australian women's team won gold medals at the 1988 and 1996 Olympic Games. The men's team won silver in 1968, 1976 and 1992, and bronze in 1964 and 1996.

Events

Event	1996 winner	2000 winner
Men's	Netherlands	
Women's	Australia	

VENUE
State Hockey Centre, Sydney Olympic Park

Judo

Judo was created in Japan in the late 19th Century. It contains elements of the fighting skills used by Samurai warriors. It became an Olympic event at the Tokyo Games in 1964. Women's events were added in 1992.

In judo, technique is more important than strength. The aim of the sport is to defeat an opponent by scoring an 'ippon' (one point). An ippon is scored when opponents are thrown onto their backs in a clean, forceful throw, or when they are kept under control by an arm-lock strangle or other legitimate hold. Men have five minutes and women four to score a point and win the contest.

OLYMPIC FACT

To qualify for the Seoul Olympic Games in 1988, gold medallist Kim Jae-yup of Korea needed to lose six kilograms in 20 days. He limited himself to one meal a day – a bowl of porridge with raw fish slices.

Extra lightweight Kye Sun (PRK) shows her gold-medal winning form at Atlanta.

Men's events

Event	1996 winner	2000 winner
Extra lightweight (60 kg)	Tadahiro Nomura (JPN)	
Half lightweight (66 kg)	Udo Quellmalz (GER)	
Lightweight (73 kg)	Kenzo Nakamura (JPN)	
Half middleweight (81 kg)	Djamel Bouras (FRA)	
Middleweight (90 kg)	Jeon Ki-Young (KOR)	
Half heavyweight (100 kg)	Pawel Nastula (POL)	
Heavyweight (100+ kg)	David Douillet (FRA)	

Women's events

Event	1996 winner	2000 winner
Extra lightweight (48 kg)	Kye Sun (PRK)	
Half lightweight (52 kg)	Marie-Claire Restoux (FRA)	
Lightweight (57 kg)	Driulis Gonzalez Morales (CUB)	
Half middleweight (63 kg)	Yuko Emoto (JPN)	
Middleweight (70 kg)	Cho Min-Sun (KOR)	
Half heavyweight (78 kg)	Ulla Werbrouck (BEL)	
Heavyweight (78+ kg)	Sun Fu-Ming (CHN)	

Half middleweight Djamel Bouras (FRA) takes gold from Toshihiko Koga (JPN) in 1996.

VENUE
Exhibition Halls 1 and 2, Darling Harbour

47

Modern Pentathlon

The five sports of modern pentathlon are shooting, fencing, swimming, showjumping and running. They represent the daring adventures of a French cavalry officer whose horse was brought down in enemy territory while he was delivering a message. He defended himself with his pistol and sword, then swam across a raging river before delivering the message on foot.

The modern pentathlon became an Olympic event in 1912. This year a women's event has been added to the program for the first time.

Alexander Parygin (KAZ), the Atlanta 1996 Olympic Games gold medallist.

Events

Event	1996 winner	2000 winner
Men's	Alexander Parygin (KAZ)	
Women's	New event	

VENUES
Shooting and fencing: Pavilion 2, Sydney Olympic Park;
Swimming: Sydney International Aquatic Centre,
Sydney Olympic Park; Showjumping and running:
Baseball Stadium, Sydney Olympic Park

Rowing

Rowing was on the program of the first Modern Olympic Games, but the races were cancelled due to bad weather. Women's events were added to the program in 1976. Rowing events are divided into lightweight and heavyweight divisions for the sculling and sweeping oar categories. In sculling events, each rower has two oars, while in sweep rowing, competitors use only one.

OLYMPIC FACT

In 1928, Australian Henry 'Bobby' Pearce stopped in the middle of his finals race to let a family of ducks pass single-file in front of his boat. He then went on to win by a five-length lead.

Kate Slatter and Megan Still (AUS) take gold in the coxless pair event at the Atlanta 1996 Olympic Games.

VENUE
Sydney International Regatta Centre, Penrith Lakes

Events

Event	1996 winner	2000 winner
Men's events		
Single scull	Switzerland	
Coxless pair	Great Britain	
Double scull	Italy	
L/w double scull	Switzerland	
Coxless four	Australia	
L/w coxless four	Denmark	
Quadruple scull	Germany	
Eight	Netherlands	
Women's events		
Single scull	Belarus	
Coxless pair	Australia	
Double scull	Canada	
L/w double scull	Romania	
Quadruple scull	Germany	
Eight	Romania	

Members of the 'Oarsome Foursome' (AUS), the Atlanta 1996 Olympic Games gold medallists in the coxless four.

Sailing

For the first time in Olympic history, sailing events (previously known as yachting) will be held close to the crowds attending the Games, rather than hundreds of kilometres away. Six courses will be used for sailing: four inside Sydney Harbour and two off the Heads. Nine classes of boat will compete.

OLYMPIC FACT

The 49er, a new class at this year's Games, is a double-handed, high performance dinghy created in Australia.

Events

Events	Class	1996 winner	2000 winner
Sailboard men's	Mistral	Greece	....
Sailboard women's	Mistral	Hong Kong	....
Singlehanded men's	Finn	Poland	....
Singlehanded women's	Europe	Denmark	....
Doublehanded men's	470	Ukraine	....
Doublehanded women's	470	Spain	....
Dinghy open	Laser	Brazil	....
High performance dinghy open	49er	New event	....
Multihull open	Tornado	Spain	....
Keelboat Fleet/ Match open	Soling	Germany	....
Keelboat open	Star	Brazil	....

VENUE
Shorebase: Sailing Marina, Rushcutters Bay; Venue: Sydney Harbour

Shooting

Shooting featured at the first Modern Olympic Games, and has had a varied program over the years. This year, there will be 17 events, for men and women. Two women's shotgun events, trap and skeet, are new to the program this year.

Events

Men's events	1996 winner	2000 winner
50 m rifle prone	Christian Klees (GER)	
50 m 3 position rifle	Jean-Pierre Amat (FRA)	
10 m air rifle	Artem Khadzhibekov (RUS)	
50 m pistol	Boris Kokorev (RUS)	
25 m rapid fire pistol	Ralf Schumann (GER)	
10 m air pistol	Roberto Di Donna (ITA)	
10 m running target	Ling Yang (CHN)	
Trap	Michael Diamond (AUS)	
Double trap	Russell Mark (AUS)	
Skeet	Ennio Falco (ITA)	

Women's events	1996 winner	2000 winner
50 m 3 position rifle	Alexandra Ivosev (YUG)	
10 m air rifle	Renata Mauer (POL)	
25 m pistol	Li Duihong (CHN)	
10 m air pistol	Olga Klochneva (RUS)	
Trap	New event	
Double trap	Kim Rhode (USA)	
Skeet	New event	

VENUE
Sydney International Shooting Centre, Cecil Park

Softball

Invented in Chicago in 1887, softball is played in more than 112 countries around the world. Early names for the game included kitten-ball and mush-ball. Fastpitch softball was included on the Olympic program for the first time in Atlanta in 1996. There will be eight teams competing this year. Only women play softball at the Olympic Games.

OLYMPIC FACT

The game is known as fastpitch due to the incredible speeds of the pitches, which average at around 100 km/hr.

Sally McDermid (AUS) slides home at Atlanta.

Events

1996 winner	2000 winner
USA	

VENUE
Softball Centre, Aquilina Reserve, Blacktown City

Table Tennis

Table tennis was invented in England in the late 1870s as an indoor alternative to lawn tennis. The game, now played in 180 countries, became part of the Olympic program in 1988.

Players need to be fit and agile and to have sharp reflexes. A point is awarded for every rally won, with the serve alternating between opponents after every five points. The winner is the first player to score 21 points.

Deng Yaping (CHN), women's singles champion in 1996.

Events

Event	1996 winner	2000 winner
Men's singles	Liu Guoliang (CHN)	....
Men's doubles	China	....
Women's singles	Deng Yaping (CHN)	....
Women's doubles	China	....

Taekwondo

Taekwondo, a martial art with traditions dating back more than 2000 years, is practised in more than 160 countries. It makes its first appearance on the Olympic program this year.

Contestants use their bare hands and feet to repel opponents. Spectacular kicking techniques used in sparring are a feature of the sport. Matches consist of three rounds of three minutes each.

An Australian team member at the National Titles, 1992.

Events

Men's events	2000 winner
Less than 58 kg	....
58–68 kg	....
68–80 kg	....
over 80 kg	....
Women's events	
Less than 49 kg	....
49–57 kg	....
57–67 kg	....
over 67 kg	....

OLYMPIC FACT

Taekwondo is a Korean word meaning 'the way of hand and foot'.

VENUE
State Sports Centre,
Sydney Olympic Park

Tennis

Although tennis was played at the first Modern Olympic Games, there were no Olympic tennis events from the 1928 to the 1984 Olympic Games.

Tennis has attracted some of the best-known athletes in the world over the last few Games, including Boris Becker, Steffi Graf, Gabriela Sabatini and the Woodies. This year's tournament will have 64 players in both the men's and women's singles, and 32 pairs in the doubles competitions. All four events will be knockout competitions.

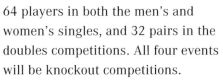

'The Woodies' (Mark Woodforde and Todd Woodbridge) (AUS), the Atlanta 1996 Olympic Games gold medallists.

Events

Event	1996 winner	2000 winner
Men's singles	Andre Agassi (USA)	
Men's doubles	Mark Woodforde/ Todd Woodbridge (AUS)	
Women's singles	Lindsay Davenport (USA)	
Women's doubles	Gigi Fernandez/ Mary Jo Fernandez (USA)	

VENUE
NSW Tennis Centre, Sydney Olympic Park

Triathlon

Triathlon developed as a sport in the United States in the 1970s, and races are now held in 105 countries around the world. This is the first year that the triathlon has appeared on the Olympic program.

The name 'triathlon' refers to the three disciplines all athletes must complete to finish a race: the swim, the cycle and the run. The Sydney Olympic course consists of a 1.5 kilometre swim in open water, a 40 kilometre bike ride and a 10 kilometre run through the centre of the city.

OLYMPIC FACT

Champion triathlete Emma Carney has won more international World Cup races and held the number one ranking longer than any other person in the history of the sport.

Champion triathlete Emma Carney (AUS) at the ITU World Cup in Sydney, 1997.

Events

Event	2000 winner
Men's triathlon	
Women's triathlon	

VENUE
Sydney Opera House forecourt

Beach Volleyball

Beach volleyball was first played on the beaches of California in the 1920s. It was recognised as an official discipline in 1986, and became an Olympic sport at Atlanta in 1996. Beach volleyball is played on a sand court by both men's and women's teams.

The court size, net height and rules of play are similar to volleyball, except that a beach volleyball team has two players rather than six.

Sachiko Fujita (JPN) competing at the Atlanta 1996 Olympic Games.

OLYMPIC FACT

American all-rounder Karch Kiraly won gold medals for regular volleyball at both the 1984 and 1988 Olympics. When beach volleyball was introduced in 1996, he scored gold yet again.

Events

Event	1996 winner	2000 winner
Men's pairs	USA	....
Women's pairs	Brazil	....

VENUE
Beach Volleyball
Centre, Bondi Beach

Volleyball

Originally called mintonette, volleyball was invented in America in 1895. The game was first played at the Olympic Games in Tokyo in 1964. Volleyball teams have six players, who change position every time their team wins back service from the opposition. Only the three players at the net positions can jump and spike or block near the net.

A new scoring system and a new specialist role, the libero, will feature at this year's competition. The libero, who will wear a different-coloured uniform from the rest of the team, will play a vital role in serve reception and backcourt defence.

Poland plays the USA at the 1996 Atlanta Olympic Games.

Events

Event	1996 winner	2000 winner
Men's	Netherlands	....
Women's	Cuba	....

VENUES
Sydney Entertainment Centre, Darling Harbour
Pavilion 4, Sydney Olympic Park

Weightlifting

In ancient Greece, lifting weights was part of an athlete's training. Weightlifting, with both one-arm and two-arm lifts, was an event in the first Modern Olympic Games. Women have been included in the program for the first time this year.

Weightlifters must complete two lifts: the snatch, and the clean and jerk. In the snatch, athletes must lift the bar to arm's length above their head in one continuous movement. In the clean and jerk, they lift the bar to their shoulders, then jerk the bar over their head, using the strength of their arms and legs. In both lifts the bar must be held overhead until the lifter is motionless.

After each successful lift, more weight is added to the bar. Athletes are given three attempts at each lift. If they fail all three, they are disqualified. Medals are awarded in each weight class for a combined total of the two lifts.

Andrej Chemerkin (RUS) takes gold in the Super Heavyweight class at Atlanta in 1996.

Men's events

Weight class	2000 winner*
56 kg	
62 kg	
69 kg	
77 kg	
85 kg	
94 kg	
105 kg	
105+ kg	

1996 Middleweight champion, Pablo Lara Rodriguez (CUB).

OLYMPIC FACT

Tiny American Charles Vinci, who won the Bantamweight gold medal at Melbourne in 1956, ran and sweated for an hour, then had a severe haircut to bring his weight down below the required limit for the competition.

Women's events

Weight class	2000 winner*
48 kg	
53 kg	
58 kg	
63 kg	
69 kg	
75 kg	
75+ kg	

*Due to changes in weight categories, 1996 winners are not listed.

VENUE
Sydney Convention Centre, Darling Harbour

Wrestling

Wrestling was the most popular sport in the Olympic Games of ancient Greece and has featured at every Modern Olympic Games, except for Paris in 1900. Wrestling is currently contested by men only at the Olympic Games.

There are two types of Olympic wrestling – freestyle and Greco-Roman. The styles share similar rules, except that Greco-Roman wrestlers can only use their arms and upper body to attack or hold, while freestyle wrestlers can also use their legs and hold their opponents above or below the waist. Technical points are awarded for various offensive and defensive holds and moves.

Super heavyweights Alexander Karelin (RUS) and Matt Ghaffari (USA) battle for gold in 1996.

OLYMPIC FACT

Kendall Cross (USA) and Giga Sissaouri (CAN) tussle for the Bantamweight gold.

Freestyle		Greco-Roman	
Event	**2000 winner***	**Event**	**2000 winner***
54 kg		54 kg	
58 kg		58 kg	
63 kg		63 kg	
69 kg		69 kg	
76 kg		76 kg	
85 kg		85 kg	
97 kg		97 kg	
130 kg		130 kg	

*Due to changes in weight categories, 1996 winners are not listed.

VENUE
Halls 1 and 2, Sydney Exhibition Centre, Darling Harbour

Nation abbreviations

AHO	Netherlands Antilles	CYP	Cyprus	KUW	Kuwait	RSA	South Africa

AHO Netherlands Antilles
ALB Albania
ALG Algeria
AND Andorra
ANG Angola
ANT Antigua and Barbuda
ARG Argentina
ARM Armenia
ARU Aruba
ASA American Samoa
AUS Australia
AUT Austria
AZE Azerbaijan
BAH Bahamas
BAN Bangladesh
BAR Barbados
BDI Burundi
BEL Belgium
BEN Benin
BER Bermuda
BHU Bhutan
BIH Bosnia and Herzegovina
BIZ Belize
BLR Belarus
BOL Bolivia
BOT Botswana
BRA Brazil
BRN Bahrain
BRU Brunei Darussalam
BUL Bulgaria
BUR Burkina Faso
CAF Central African Republic
CAM Cambodia
CAN Canada
CAY Cayman Islands
CGO Congo
CHA Chad
CHI Chile
CHN People's Republic of China
CIS Commonwealth of Independent States, 1992
CIV Côte d'Ivoire
CMR Cameroon
COD Democratic Republic of the Congo
COK Cook Islands
COL Colombia
COM Comoros
CPV Cape Verde
CRC Costa Rica
CRO Croatia
CUB Cuba

CYP Cyprus
CZE Czech Republic
DEN Denmark
DJI Djibouti
DMA Dominica
DOM Dominican Republic
ECU Ecuador
EGY Egypt
ERI Eritrea
ESA El Salvador
ESP Spain
EST Estonia
ETH Ethiopia
FIJ Fiji
FIN Finland
FRA France
FSM Federated States of Micronesia
GAB Gabon
GAM Gambia
GBR Great Britain
GBS Guinea-Bissau
GDR East Germany (1949–1990)
GEO Georgia
GEQ Equatorial Guinea
GER Germany
GHA Ghana
GRE Greece
GRN Grenada
GUA Guatemala
GUI Guinea
GUM Guam
GUY Guyana
HAI Haiti
HKG Hong Kong, China
HON Honduras
HUN Hungary
INA Indonesia
IND India
IRI Islamic Republic of Iran
IRL Ireland
IRQ Iraq
ISL Iceland
ISR Israel
ISV Virgin Islands
ITA Italy
IVB British Virgin Islands
JAM Jamaica
JOR Jordan
JPN Japan
KAZ Kazakstan
KEN Kenya
KGZ Kyrgyzstan
KOR Korea
KSA Saudi Arabia

KUW Kuwait
LAO Lao People's Democratic Republic
LAT Latvia
LBA Libyan Arab Jamahiriya
LBR Liberia
LCA Saint Lucia
LES Lesotho
LIB Lebanon
LIE Liechtenstein
LTU Lithuania
LUX Luxembourg
MAD Madagascar
MAR Morocco
MAS Malaysia
MAW Malawi
MDA Republic of Moldova
MDV Maldives
MEX Mexico
MGL Mongolia
MKD Former Yugoslav Republic of Macedonia
MLI Mali
MLT Malta
MON Monaco
MOZ Mozambique
MRI Mauritius
MTN Mauritania
MYA Myanmar
NAM Namibia
NCA Nicaragua
NED Netherlands
NEP Nepal
NGR Nigeria
NIG Niger
NOR Norway
NRU Nauru
NZL New Zealand
OMA Oman
PAK Pakistan
PAN Panama
PAR Paraguay
PER Peru
PHI Philippines
PLE Palestine
PLW Palau
PNG Papua New Guinea
POL Poland
POR Portugal
PRK Democratic People's Republic of Korea
PUR Puerto Rico
QAT Qatar
ROM Romania

RSA South Africa
RUS Russian Federation
RWA Rwanda
SAM Samoa
SEN Senegal
SEY Seychelles
SIN Singapore
SKN Saint Kitts and Nevis
SLE Sierra Leone
SLO Slovenia
SMR San Marino
SOL Soloman Islands
SOM Somalia
SRI Sri Lanka
STP Sao Tome and Principe
SUD Sudan
SUI Switzerland
SUR Suriname
SVK Slovakia
SWE Sweden
SWZ Swaziland
SYR Syrian Arab Republic
TAN United Republic of Tanzania
TCH Czechoslovakia (to 1993)
TGA Tonga
THA Thailand
TJK Tajikistan
TKM Turkmenistan
TOG Togo
TPE Chinese Taipei
TRI Trinidad and Tobago
TUN Tunisia
TUR Turkey
UAE United Arab Emirates
UGA Uganda
UKR Ukraine
URS Soviet Union (to 1992)
URU Uruguay
USA United States of America
UZB Uzbekistan
VAN Vanuatu
VEN Venezuela
VIE Vietnam
VIN Saint Vincent and the Grenadines
YEM Yemen
YUG Yugoslavia
ZAM Zambia
ZIM Zimbabwe

Penguin Books Ltd, Melbourne, London, New York, Toronto,
Auckland, South Africa, India

First published by Penguin Books Australia, 2000
This edition © Penguin Books Australia Ltd
487 Maroondah Highway, PO Box 257
Ringwood, Victoria 3134, Australia

TM © SOCOG 1996

The publishers have made every effort to ensure that the information
in this book was correct at the time of publication.

SOCOG takes no responsibility for information that becomes outdated
after publication. For the latest information, visit SOCOG on the
World Wide Web at www.olympics.com

Written and compiled by Meredith Costain
Designed by Lynn Twelftree
Typeset in Binary ITC, Corporate ABQ 10pt, News Gothic
Printed and bound through Bookbuilders

National Library of Australia
Cataloguing-in-Publication data:
Sydney 2000 Olympic Games

ISBN 0 7214 8889 7.

Olympic Games (27th : Sydney, N.S.W.) –
Miscellanea. 2. Olympics – Records. 3. Olympics – History.

796.48

ACKNOWLEDGEMENTS
Front cover photographs:
Top: John Carnemolla/Allsport
Centre: Duane Hart/Sporting Images
Bottom, centre: Mike Powell/Allsport USA
Bottom, right: DavidCannon/Allsport
Back cover photograph: Mike Powell/Allsport
Text photographs: Sport the Library
Main photo, pp. 6/7: Otto Rogge/Stock Photos Pty Ltd
Photographs of Stadium Australia – The Olympic Stadium on p.7
and Foldout authorised by Stadium Australia
Main photograph, Venues Foldout:
Image courtesy of Olympic Coordination Authority (OCA)